THE WILD
KEEPS HER HOLY

POEMS

TIFFANY AURORA

BOOKS OF POETRY
BY TIFFANY AURORA

Sunrise Eyes & Hallelujah Breath (2020)
There Is Always Universe: Poems (2019)

Available worldwide on Amazon
& Book Depository .com

Copyright ©2018 Tiffany Aurora
All rights reserved. ISBN:172001308X
Poems, book, cover design, & concept
by Tiffany Aurora
Instagram: @tiffany.aurora.poetry
Facebook: Tiffany Aurora Poetry

Cover photo by: JP Longmeadow
Instagram: @longmeadowphoto
Facebook: JP Longmeadow

Edited by: Saide Harb-Ranero
Instagram: @rappaccinis.daughter
& K.K. Foster
Instagram: @kkfosterlyrics

FOREWARD

THE WILD KEEPS HER HOLY,
is first & foremost stemmed from the grief of my
journey out of the mormon church, after being a
lifelong member & surviving & coming to terms
with ongoing abuse that happened in a religious
setting, as a young teenager. This collection contains
some pieces of a sensitive nature relating to abuse,
mental health, & also more adult pieces, which may
be triggering for some readers & not age
appropriate for others. Please proceed with the
ultimate self-care in mind.

If you aren't already familiar with my work, I use
unconventional punctuation & dashes to signify
pauses & breaths. I love word art & throwing my
favorite movie & music references into my poems. I
try to write about the loss & grief of losing my
religion, in a way that is relatable to anyone who has
experienced a heartbreak or loss in their lives. Some
poems are long & some are short. This collection is
intended to be read in one healing sitting, & the
poems are placed to flow with the changing seasons.

Never give up. Keep searching for the light. Because
it will never stop searching for you. I thank you for
reading. Remember beautiful survivor, you are
never ever, ever alone.

To all who have ever
lost & found themselves again.
These words are for you.

CONTENTS

SCREAM

Be patient
with yourself.
You are slowly
coming home
to your own heart.
It whispers
as it waits.
Even when you
scream back
that you are
a nameless wanderer
who answers to
no one.

ALLEGIANCE

I don't know
the exact moment
my heart stopped
beating for you
and turned it's
allegiance to me—
but I do know
survival was
deeply involved
in the process
of it all.

THE CHAOS WITHIN ME

I was not born to
k n e e l t o
the chaos within me—
I was born to
r u l e i t.

A HYMN FOR BROKENNESS

If I could but
reach my hand
into my chest.
Stroke the flesh
of brain & breast.
Piece by piece
to realign—
each broken bit
of heart & mind.

BEAUTIFUL POSSIBILITIES

I look at
broken things
& all my
eyes & heart
can see are
beautiful possibilities.

MUSTARD SEEDS

R I V E R S
can find
the ocean
eventually.
It is the reason
I have to believe
that each tear
the stars have
cried for us—
will finally
amount to
enough water
to cut through
the mountains
we have not yet
been able to move—
by putting our trust
in faith alone.
*(We tried our best to be
mustard seeds didn't we?)*

JOURNEY

Never
question your journey
because
someone else does.

THE TREE OF ME

Please build your nest
in the tree of me.

There is light
in this heart.

There is love
in this being.

UMBRELLA

I cried more
than the rain today
& your love was
the perfect umbrella.

I AM HERE TO TELL YOU

I am here to tell you—
that I know what it is like
to take a living,
breathing heart,
bury it in the ground
& cover it with the dirt
you think you are.

I am here to tell you—
that the hurting will
come back to haunt you.
When it does
you must let it go.

I am here to tell you—
that shattered things
can be put back together
in the most peculiar
& beautiful of ways.

I am here to tell you—
that you are fixable.

LITTLE PLACES

Beautiful
things
bloom
in
the
most
b r o k e n
little
places.

BONES

Now that
you are gone—
I think I understand
the reason why
hearts do not
have bones.

WITHOUT HANDS

& somehow.
Even without hands—
the heart it holds on.
& on & on & on & on
& on & on & on & on
& on & on & on & on
& on & on & on & on
& on & on & on & on
& on & on & on & on
& on & on & on & on
& on & on & on & on
& on & on & on & on
& on & on & on & on
& on & on & on & on
& on & on & on & on
& on & on & on & on
& on & on & on & on
& on & on & on & on
& on & on & on & on
& on & on & on & on
& on & on & on & on
& on & on & on & on.

HOPE

H o p e
is always
the best place
to start.

GRAPEVINE

You plucked
my heart
like a grape
from the vine.
Crushing it between
your teeth
as you bit down
on goodbyes so firmly—
you permanently crippled
your own tongue.

PUSH

Push me in
I will swim away.
Let me dive—
I am here
to stay.

FROM WHAT GREAT HEIGHTS

I climbed the walls
you built today.
Bent the knees
that would not pray.
Caught the meaning
in your words.
With broken wings
flew with the birds.
I dare not share
the sights I saw.
Or from what great heights
I had to fall.
To knock my heart
into my teeth
& kiss the wounds
that lie beneath.

STRAWBERRY MOON

We fuck to prove
we're still alive—
under a strawberry moon
& jealous sky.

PHOENIX IN JULY

The truths of life
are hard to swallow sometimes.
Like tortilla chips slowly scratching
their way down your throat.
Like someone trying to teach you
how to swim on dry land.
Like phoenix in July with no water.
Like the wiggly squeak wheeled
shopping cart you chose—
instead of the hundreds of others
that glide elegantly, into any room
without turning heads.
Like mouths that have
such a way with words—
but end up tongue tied & parched
in the moments they should be
showering others with gratitude.
Like staying up all night
to see the eclipse—
but ten minutes before dawn
the only storm cloud in sight
has blocked out the heavens.
Like saying, "hello,"
but really meaning,
"goodbye."
Like flying flat footed,
upon this grand earth—
but walking the infinite skies.

PLUNGE

If I

p
l
u
n
g
e

any deeper
into the watery
graves of you—
I fear I will

d
r
o
w
n
us both.

IMPOSSIBLE GAMES

Some hearts
are just impossible games—
that can never be won
no matter how perfectly
you play by their rules.

STUCK

If you are not
beginning—
then you are not
moving.
If you are not
moving—
then you are
{stuck} waiting.
If you are
{stuck} waiting—
then you are
losing something.
If you are
losing something—
then you should
go back
to the beginning.
If you are back
at the beginning—
then this could be
the end.

NEVER ENDING STORIES

"I had to take everything
from you as quickly as I could—
so you couldn't take it
from me first," you said.

footstep
footstep
footstep
click
creak
slam
heaving breaths
*pitch **black***

"Why is it so **dark**?"
Heartbreak screams.

Hope whispers—

"A wise empress once said—
'In the beginning, it is always **dark**.' "

makes wish

"Make me whole without you. Please."

LIGHTHOUSE

Let these eyes
be a lighthouse.

Let these arms
be a safe harbor.

Let this heart
be a long awaited shore.

A WILDFLOWER WITH NO NAME

What place is this?
Here I sit,
caught somewhere
before the lavender
& after the tulips.
An unwanted seed,
growing in an
uncharted season.
Longing for a
garden of eden
where I am not
cast out for
the sole reason of
 being what I have
always been since I
came into this world:
a wildflower with no name.

PRACTICE

Oh yes,
it will take some practice.
This: letting go of things
that are no longer good
for my heart.

FOREIGN OBJECTS

I have tried to
dislodge us
from my heart—
but it seems my soul
is not properly trained
in the removal of
foreign objects
that still feel
so very much
like home.

FIX

Some people
get high
on goodbyes—
& we keep
letting them
get their fix—
because we like
to stay drunk
on empty promises.

UNLEARNING YOU

I
cannot
unlearn
you.
For
you
taught
me
your
heart
too
well.

THE MISSING

There is
so much missing
in my heart today—
& it is the worst
kind of missing
one can do.
The kind
where people
stay missing
on purpose—
because they don't
know how to tell you
that they feel
the missing
too.

THE UPSIDE
TO THE UPSIDE-DOWN

We agreed that
we had been turned
UPSIDE-DOWN.
That we might be
gone for good—
but this is love
& stranger things
have happened
when they should.

BURN

Let's burn the wild
into our bones—
until we are
one melted flesh.

BROKEN HEART TOOK ALL
(I KNOW)

I know that pain,
I know that fall.
I know that look of
broken heart took all.

I know the sorrow, the inner brawl.
of plugging your ears to someone's call.
Then spirit shattered, be forced to crawl.
'Cause it's, keep on movin'
or it's freeze for the fucking long haul.

But.

I know how to hold on,
I know how to let go—
I know who to keep,
& I know who to throw.

I know how to love,
I know how to hate—
I know how to forgive.
I know when to forsake.

I know when to jump ship,
I know when to steer sharp.
I know when to be soft,
I know when to fight hard.

BITTERSWEET

The flavor
of a love left
untasted—
is always the most
bittersweet.

ROCKY PEAKS

Your
rocky peaks
I cannot climb—
both on foot
& in my mind.

(I Wish You Never Chose To Leave This World.)

In loving memory of J. P. P. R. J.

National Suicide Prevention Lifeline:
1-800-273-8255

SEAS OF BRINE

You slipped away
like seas of brine.
Between fingers
stretched wide.
Gentle & weightless—
& my hands, my hands,
they dried much too quickly.
I cannot help but swirl my tongue
against the ghostly oceans of you—
still lingering upon my skin.

LIKE A SUMMER EVENING

Echo softly
on the water.
Whisper sweetly
through the pines.
Love me like a
summer evening.
We'll pretend that
you're still mine.

AMBER'S POEM

I am
the dreamer
& the doer.
I am
the stayer,
the shaker,
the mover.
I am
the softness
& the strength.
I am the depth,
of the width,
of the length.
I am
the beggar
& the chooser.
I am
the winner
& the loser.
I am
the day
as much as
the night.
I am
all wrong—
& therefore
just right.

SPARK

She was a spark—
forever in love
with the wind.

ALPINE LOOP

Driving in loops around alpines.
Circling back on memories
that do not yellow with age,
do not fizzle with time.
I still dip your name in sweet pea
& breathe it into the summer wind—
send it echoing through the trees,
a top seven little peaks
that would still break my heart
if I dared to climb them.

DEAD MEN TELL PLENTY OF TALES

"Dead men tell no tales,"
they say.
But I write down
your ghost stories
every day.

YOU KNOW WHO YOU ARE

Maybe now
that many years
have passed—
you will read this
& understand
what I meant,
what I mean,
what I will always
be meaning
when I write us down:
the poetry is all you have left of me.

(You know who you are.)

NAKED SOUL

Let go of a love
that does not
honor & crave
your naked soul.

PERMANENT INK

Names should not be
written across the sky
in permanent ink
if they can never truly
belong to us.
But I guess that is
what one does
when falling in love
with a different kind
of stardust.
We try to make
forever last in
any way we can.

YOU LEFT LIKE THE WIND

No matter
how many times
I remind myself
that one cannot
hold hands with
the wind—
these fingers still
reach for your own.

NOWHERE OVER THE RAINBOW

Once upon a rainbow
we felt like a promise.
Now we are lost in
some deadly desert.
Walking yellow brick roads,
embedded with fools gold.
Wandering aimlessly toward
emerald tinted memories.
There is no such place as,
"Home," anymore.
Not in the story of us.
You can't come back,
you don't know how it works.
This life. This love.
This heart. This truth.
This wanting the things—
that have always
wanted you.

YOUNG, WILD, & UNAFRAID

Sometimes
I wonder what it
would have been like—
to love you in the way
I truly wanted to:
young, wild, & unafraid.

SEA-LOVE POEM

Your skin
is a swim
in the ocean.

A bask
in the gentlest
of waves.

The most
precious of all
hidden treasure.

From dark
& mysterious
caves.

ABSENCE

In some places
I still don't know
where you end
& I begin.
But slowly,
in your absence—
I am learning.

SILVER LINING

The moon
promises to keep
all of our secrets.
It watches
as we grab our
silver lining—
pull it all the way
up to our ears,
& tuck ourselves in
for the rest of always.

SOFT HEART

It is a
hard thing
at times—
having such
a very
soft heart.

SUNSHINE & CHEAP PERFUME

I flip the switch.
Look at you with eyes
that scream,
"Let's make this room smell like
sunshine & cheap perfume."
(So we do.)

THIS IS A POEM THAT NEVER ENDS

So here is
the problem.

To think of you—
means living & dying
all at once.

So here is
the problem.

To not think of you—
means living & dying
all at once.

So here is
the problem.

(This Is A Poem That Never Ends.)

ASHES

You light me up
again & again—
only to walk away
from the flame.
Even our **ashes**
still get me high.

SLEEPING IN OAK TREES

Sleeping in oak trees—
atop branches full of nets
made clumsily but strong
(like the two of us)
& could bear the weight
of all the things we'd never say.
Under a sky filled with stars
we dangled our hearts
from the leaves as
wildly {carelessly}
as the love written
all over our faces.
We created many things
that I still keep—
because you are just
a ghost story who will
never come back for them.

ROOM

This life is not a
one size fits all—
& that is why we must
make room
for each other.

UNTAMED CREATURE

I have worn my feet to the bone
roaming the wilderness for you—
& succeeded only in turning this heart
into the most untamed creature
ever to wander the earth.

FLIGHT

We scream
in whispers.
Stomp as
we tiptoe.
Keep secrets
as good as
jet planes
in the night.
Weigh ourselves
d
o
w
n
with feathers
that should be
flying us over
endless love
& potential.
Yet.
We wonder why
we never take
flight.

AIMLESSLY

Perhaps
you do not need to
wander aimlessly
in order to be found
& it is just that you
have not yet made
what you hold
in your hands
into a true home.

CALL

Even the wildest
of things can
come back to us—
if our hearts will
only learn how to
call them home.

OCTOBER

October
will always belong
to the way you
held my hand.

BINDING SPELL

The quiet
within the quiet,
that is where
you'll find me.
The space between
the light & **dark**,
that is where
I bind me.

RED SEAS

If only our tears
ran red like blood—
perhaps then all our lips
would speak a little bit kinder.

I AM NOVEMBER

Standing restlessly
on the border
of two foreign countries
that do not want me—
I am November
naked hearted & gray.
Always between seasons.
Aching for breaths
from autumn-ed lips
that sigh for these kisses
no more.

SHIVER

Lips & heart
still quiver.
Still shiver—
at the sound
of your name.

MEMORY LANE

For you
I not only walk down
memory lane—
I do it barefoot.
On hot coals.
At snail's pace.
Naked.
In the dead
of winter.

SIDEWAYS

We fucked
each other
sideways.
Like the
blowing snow.
Like the
raging blizzards
that we were.

LIKE THE WINTER

I still wear you
like the winter—
in *so many layers.*

CONVERSATIONS
WITH DEPRESSION

"Do you want
to come out?
Spend some time
where it's light?"

"No," she replied.
"I'm in love
with the night."

SAY IT WITH ME

"I am no longer
what happened to me.
I am now what happened
after what happened to me,
finally healed."

WORLD MAP

I have cried enough oceans—
to be worthy of a spot
on the world map.
I have typed enough letters—
to build a mountain,
out the hurt(s)
&, 'I don't know any mores.'
I have walked enough miles on eggshells—
that I will spend years healing my raw feet.
I have learned how to mend a broken heart
so many times, it is a wonder
that it still finds a way
to beat louder & stronger
with each shattering.

THE SECRET TO HEALING

I am going to tell you
the secret to healing:

<u>HONOR</u> <u>THE</u> <u>THINGS</u>
<u>YOU</u> <u>ONCE</u> <u>BURIED</u>.

IN-BETWEEN

No longer
winter.
Not quite
spring.
Broken
but
healing.
She's
in-between.

GRAVEYARD NO MORE

I am awake now.
Listening to the woman
inside of my bones.
Finishing her
'undone(s).'
All the raw
& beautiful things
she buried deep
within her heart.
I have dug them up.
We are graveyard no more.

TULIP IN THE SNOW

She peeked out her head,
looked to and fro.
Felt a bite.
(Late winter snows.)
The day was bright,
blue skies above.
The time had come
to sprout her buds.
Should she recoil
beneath the ground?
Or keep her head up
loud & proud?
She brushed off the ice,
let her petals undone.
Took a big drink of brave
& made friends with the sun.

DAMN HOW

These wings are
scarred and dirty—
but damn how
they've learned
to fly.

THE LITTLE LIES
WE TELL OURSELVES

~~I didn't.~~
~~I used to.~~
~~I don't.~~
Fuck.
I still do.
I love you.

NO LONGER

I will no longer
break my own heart—
to pacify
the egos of others.

ALWAYS-LAND

Second star
to the left
& straight on
'til midnight.
That is where
I will not love you.
That is where
I will never wait.

COMPASS

Take courage.
Wrap your arms
around fear.
Stop it from
quaking.
You are an
endless vessel
of love & possibilities.
Doubt belongs nowhere
near the compass of
your heart.

SWALLOWS

Wait for a love
that swallows
you whole—
but allows you
to keep all
that you are.

THE KEEPING KIND

I wont let you
lose you.
I wont let you
lose me—
& that is what
makes us
the keeping kind.

WORTHY

You are WORTHY.

Of love.
(The kindest, with the purest of intentions.)

Of yourself.
(All that you were, are, & have yet to become.)

Of beautiful friendships.
(The kind that encourage you to bloom,
even when you are trapped beneath
the cold, hard dirt of doubt.)

You are WORTHY.

Of being heard.
(Your words, your voice, your soft heart.)

Do you hear me?

You are WORTHY.

SAFER

Are we safer
in the arms of those
we ought to leave behind?
Or delaying the inevitable
& running out of time?

SOME DAYS

Some days
I think of us—
& it hurts
remembering
just how
f a r   o f f
you have gone
since loving me.

Some days
I think of us—
& smile at
remembering
just how
f a r   b a c k
I have come
since loving you.

SAFE PLACE

Love should feel
like the safest place
your heart
has ever been.

MATTER UNORGANIZED

We are beautiful chaos,
that may never make sense.

Matter unorganized.

But.

We are love.
We are truth.
We are ours.
We are free.

PERMANENCE

Let the
softness
be **permanent.**

Let the
permanence
be soft.

CLIMB

If home is where the heart is—
then I must learn to
climb inside your chest.

WAITING FOR YOU

It is enough for now—
to love you from here.
To sit in the quiet
with gentle anticipation—
of the finding you are doing
inside of that skin.
One day soon
I will see you again.

THE WAY BACK TO NOW

We look so hard
at the road   ahead—
we forget to see
where it has
already led.

ROOT

Someone once
asked me
how they would know
that the healing
was starting to take root
& I told them,
"When THE END—
finally feels like
the beginning."

<u>ACKNOWLEDGMENTS</u>

Attention my dear husband
& my beautiful children.
Thank you.
For supporting my heart
& art with your love, never ending patience,
& belief in me. I love you.

Thank you to all the beautiful humans
transitioning in their faiths & life paths,
who have told me your stories of
heartbreak, healing, & love.
You have inspired my own heart
& journey so very much.
I am thankful for you all. You are so brave.
Lighter days are coming.

Thank you to my darling tribe of kindreds.
I love you so much.
Your friendship, encouragement, & inspiration
means the world to me.
I don't plan to ever do life without you.

Finally, thank you to loss.
For without it, these words would not exist.

ABOUT THE AUTHOR

Tiffany Aurora is originally from
Southern California & now resides in
the Rocky Mountains
with her husband, children, and their dogs.
She loves to drink tea any time of day
& has a great love for all things Harry Potter.
Currently Aurora is working on her
next collection of poetry
& her first fantasy fiction trilogy.

Find Tiffany across social media where she holds a
following of over 100K readers:
Instagram: @tiffany.aurora.poetry
Facebook: Tiffany Aurora Poetry
Pinterest: Tiffany Aurora Poetry
Instagram: @a.wildflower.with.no.name
Facebook: A Wildflower With No Name
Facebook: Nature Poetry & Quotes
Facebook: Barefoot In The Lavender

Made in the USA
Las Vegas, NV
25 February 2021

18598968R00059